"I Have a Dream"

A 50TH YEAR TESTAMENT
TO THE MARCH THAT CHANGED AMERICA

A Southern Christian Leadership Conference
Commemorative Photo Journal

By the Southern Christian Leadership Conference
Photographs by Bob Adelman

Dr. Bernard LaFayette, Jr., Chairman
Dr. Charles Steele, Chief Executive Officer
Damien Conners, Executive Director
Dr. Rodney Sampson, Publisher, eDNA Press

Vice President, Publisher: Tim Moore
Associate Publisher and Director of Marketing: Amy Neidlinger
Development Editor: Russ Hall
Operations Specialist: Jodi Kemper
Marketing Manager: Lisa Loftus
Cover Designer: Alan Clements
Managing Editor: Kristy Hart
Senior Project Editor: Lori Lyons
Copy Editor: Karen Gill dba Gill Editorial Services
Proofreader: Paula Lowell
Interior Designer: Kim Scott, Bumpy Design
Compositor: Kim Scott, Bumpy Design
Photo Scanning: Steven D. Morse
Graphics Technician: Tammy Graham
Manufacturing Buyer: Dan Uhrig

Pearson offers excellent discounts on this book when ordered in quantity for bulk purchases or special sales. For more information, please contact U.S. Corporate and Government Sales, 1-800-382-3419, corpsales@pearsontechgroup.com. For sales outside the U.S., please contact International Sales at international@pearsoned.com.

The March Itself: Photographs and Captions © Bob Adelman

Company and product names mentioned herein are the trademarks or registered trademarks of their respective owners.

Printed in the United States of America

First Printing August 2013

ISBN-10: 0-13-349839-5
ISBN-13: 978-0-13-349839-4

Pearson Education LTD.
Pearson Education Australia PTY, Limited.
Pearson Education Singapore, Pte. Ltd.
Pearson Education Asia, Ltd.
Pearson Education Canada, Ltd.
Pearson Educación de Mexico, S.A. de C.V.
Pearson Education—Japan
Pearson Education Malaysia, Pte. Ltd.

Library of Congress Control Number: 2013940205

TABLE OF CONTENTS

FOREWORD

By Dr. Bernard LaFayette, Chairman,
Southern Christian Leadership Conference

On August 28, a Wednesday in 1963, something quite amazing occurred. In the photo journal that follows, you can experience that event that changed America.

African American civil rights organizations, including the Negro American Labor Council, the National Association for the Advancement of Colored People (NAACP), the Student Nonviolent Coordinating Committee, the Congress of Racial Equality, and the National Urban League united into joint leadership, with Dr. Martin Luther King, Jr. and the Southern Christian Leadership Conference (SCLC) prominent among them, in one of the largest political rallies ever to march on Washington, D.C. on behalf of their civil and economic rights.

And the nation listened.

Some say it was Mahalia Jackson who called out from the crowd for King to "Tell them about the dream." He did.

In a seventeen-minute speech in which he diverted from his notes, Dr. King gave one of the most stirring speeches in the history of America. Standing in front of the Lincoln Memorial, he delivered his "I Have a Dream" speech, in which he advocated racial and economic harmony.

Estimates vary on the number of participants in the march, but most reports agree on around a quarter of a million people, most black, but with white, Jewish, and nonblack minority supporters.

The march, made 100 years after the Emancipation Proclamation, was organized to encourage jobs and freedom. It is widely credited with helping to pass the Civil Rights Act (1964) and the Voting Rights Act (1965).

America had indeed listened.

INTRODUCTION

ALMOST EVERYONE HAS HEARD OF the "American Dream," wherein all people have an equal opportunity to advance and improve their lot through education and hard work. In the early days of America, though, that simply did not exist for most African Americans.

The root of the problem existed initially with slavery, an institution that had been around for ages and had been prevalent across the globe. The Greeks, the Romans, and even the Africans themselves practiced a form of it, although these early forms of slavery and indentured servitude didn't compare with the brutality and human degradation instituted by chattel slavery in America. Although the Hammurabic Code, dating back to the Babylonian times, provided for the eventual liberation of slaves, many civilizations were far from being that understanding.

The Portuguese and Spanish brought what we know as African slavery to Europe in the mid-fifteenth century. In the early sixteenth century, the Spanish brought the first African slave to Mexico, and later to Cuba. So, upon the discovery of the New World, a land of opportunity and freedom from religious persecution for many, the first Africans to arrive there in the mid-1600s did so as slaves.

There is little doubt that slavery was a huge economic driver, but was it right? Was it just?

Christianity, and the enlightenment it brought, would in time heighten the moral conscience to stir many in the North to moral outrage enough to lead to one of the bloodiest and most brutal of wars, the Civil War, and from it the Emancipation Proclamation.

But a proclamation of equal rights was not enough to make it so. For 100 years following, America would struggle with biases and prejudices of the past that restricted the rights—civil and economic—of African Americans.

It would take a heroic effort by African Americans to stand up to the rest of America and declare that the time had come to open the American Dream to all. That effort reached its peak on August 28, 1963, when Dr. Martin Luther King, Jr. and the SCLC were in the forefront of a march of around a quarter of a million Americans, largely African Americans, on Washington, D.C.

The photos and narrative that follow share what led to that event, the event itself, and what came after, letting you share a more intimate feel for *The March That Changed America.*

THE EARLIEST DAYS

THE ROAD TO A CAUSE OR PURPOSE BEGINS with a need to fix an injustice. In a country with freedom and equality among its bywords, inequality and injustice existed nevertheless, and these wrongs would take a long time to right. For African Americans, it was a journey that had to be made—one that no one could make for them, and one that would be made against opposition, and because of opposition. It is a story in which Dr. Martin Luther King, Jr. and the Southern Christian Leadership Conference (SCLC) played a vital part. This is the story of that long path through destiny, through adversity, and to victory.

Somber Days for Humanity

The starkest form of injustice is the entrapment and slavery of a people. From the earliest times in America, slavery was an accepted practice, one employed and endorsed by some of the country's founding fathers. A quarter of a century before American independence, slavery was legal in all 13 colonies, and as many as 12 million slaves were brought to the Americas from the sixteenth through the nineteenth centuries, with nearly 700,000 coming to what is now the United States.[1] Spain and England were major participants in the African slave trade. Sir Francis Drake and associates helped establish the "slave triangle," a circuit from West Africa through the Caribbean to Europe where slaves were exchanged for cash crops and manufactured goods. The growth continued until the profits of the slave trade and West Indian plantations represented 5% of the British economy by the time of the Industrial Revolution.[2]

The slave era was a low ebb in humanity, with couples and families divided and sold in public squares to live far apart, never to see each other again. This was as far from freedom and equality as life can get, and it was going to be a long time before things changed.

There are almost no positive moments among a practice where the shipping to the Americas alone had a mortality rate of around 15%.[3] The slave mutiny on the schooner *La Amistad* in 1839 that led to a Supreme Court case in 1841, where John Quincy Adams argued on behalf of the Africans and won, was one of the few bright moments in a somber period for America.

Adams was not the only American to begin to have doubts about the morality and rightness of slavery. Those opposed to slavery began to be known as "abolitionists." These people existed mainly in the northern states, because following Eli Whitney's invention of the cotton gin, cotton became the chief crop of the South, amounting to the bulk of all its exports. The cheap labor of owning slaves was the most cost-effective way of producing cotton. Although the owners of huge plantations did not represent a majority in the South, they were the political leaders and knew what drove their economy. For their economic and political success, plantation owners of the South felt the institution of slavery had to continue, whereas many in the North would come to have an opposing view. A rift between the thinking of the northern and southern states continued to be an ominous factor, one with all the power and ferocity of a ticking bomb.

As of 1850, Congress passed the Fugitive Slave Act, which required individuals to return runaway slaves to their owners. In direct opposition, the Underground Railroad would operate at its peak from 1850 to 1860. Founded by ex-slave Harriet Tubman and supported in part by the Quakers and abolitionists, including John Brown, the Underground Railroad was composed of a network of secretive routes and safe houses where a growing number of abolitionists and other sympathizers helped slaves escape to the free states, Mexico, or Canada, where slavery was prohibited.

The Dred Scott Decision of 1857 only deepened the rift between the free states of the North and the slave states of the South. He sued for his freedom on the basis that he and his wife Harriet and two daughters had lived with his master Dr. Emerson in a free state. Scott's temporary residence outside Missouri did not bring about his emancipation under the Missouri Compromise, which the Supreme Court ruled unconstitutional because it would improperly deprive Scott's owner of his legal property. The Court also found that neither he nor any other person of African ancestry could claim citizenship in the United States; therefore, Scott could not bring suit in federal court. Chief Justice Roger B. Taney had hoped to settle the issues related to slavery and Congressional authority by this decision, yet it only aroused greater public outrage and deepened sectional tensions between the northern and southern U.S. states until the decision was later overturned by the Emancipation Proclamation.

One indication of how deep and fanatical the rift had grown came in 1859 when John Brown and his group of radical abolitionists raided the arsenal at Harper's Ferry in an attempt to start an armed slave revolt. He had invited Harriet Tubman and Fredrick Douglass to join him. Tubman was ill, and Douglass did not believe the raid would succeed. He was right. Brown was later hung after his unsuccessful efforts.

The issue of slavery and rights of blacks in America became the driving reason for the Civil War. Those in the South were angered at the attempts by Northern antislavery political forces to block the expansion of slavery into the western territories, feeling that a restriction on slavery would violate the principle of states' rights. When Abraham Lincoln won the 1860 presidential election, in spite of not being on the ballot in ten Southern states, his victory triggered declarations of secession by seven slave states in the South. They formed the Confederate States of America before Lincoln even took office. Nationalists (in the North and elsewhere), in addition to foreign governments, refused to recognize the secessions, and the U.S. government in Washington refused to abandon its forts that were in territory claimed by the Confederacy. War began in April 1861 when Confederates attacked Fort Sumter, a U.S. fortress in South Carolina, the state that had been the first to declare its independence. The Civil War began in earnest.

Although they waged one of the bloodiest wars in history—one that split families and states as well as the North and South—steps began to be taken to deal with the issue of slavery itself. In January 1862, Thaddeus Stevens, the Republican leader in the House of Representatives, called for the total war against the rebellion to include the emancipation of slaves. He argued that emancipation, by forcing the loss of enslaved labor, would ruin the rebel economy.

In July 1862, Lincoln first discussed the proclamation with his Cabinet. He believed he needed a Union victory on the battlefield so that his decision would appear positive and strong. That came on September 22, 1862, with the Battle of Antietam, in which Union troops turned back a Confederate invasion of Maryland. This gave Lincoln his opportunity. Lincoln told Cabinet members that he had made a covenant with God, that if the Union drove the Confederacy out of Maryland, he would issue the Emancipation Proclamation. Five days after Antietam, Lincoln called his Cabinet into session and issued the Preliminary Proclamation. Congress followed that announcement by passing in July 1862 the Second Confiscation Act, containing provisions intended to liberate slaves held by "rebels." Lincoln then signed it into law.

THE EMANCIPATION PROCLAMATION

PRESIDENT ABRAHAM LINCOLN issued the Emancipation Proclamation on January 1, 1863. The nation was about to enter its third year of bloody civil war. The proclamation declared "that all persons held as slaves" within the rebellious states "are, and henceforward shall be free."

Despite the wording, the Emancipation Proclamation was limited in many ways. It applied only to states that had seceded from the Union, leaving slavery untouched in the loyal border states. It also exempted parts of the Confederacy that had already come under Northern control. Also, the freedom it promised depended on Union military victory.

Although the Emancipation Proclamation did not end slavery in the nation, it captured the hearts and emotions of millions of Americans and fundamentally transformed the character of the war.

Every advance of federal troops after January 1, 1863 expanded the domain of freedom. The Proclamation also announced the acceptance of black men into the Union Army and Navy, enabling the liberated to become liberators. By the end of the war, almost 200,000 black soldiers and sailors had fought for the Union and freedom.

Transcript of the Emancipation Proclamation, January 1, 1863

By the President of the United States of America: A Proclamation.

Whereas, on the twenty-second day of September, in the year of our Lord one thousand eight hundred and sixty-two, a proclamation was issued by the President of the United States, containing, among other things, the following, to wit:

That on the first day of January, in the year of our Lord one thousand eight hundred and sixty-three, all persons held as slaves within any State or designated part of a State, the people whereof shall then be in rebellion against the United States, shall be then, thenceforward, and forever free; and the Executive Government of the United States, including the military and naval authority thereof, will recognize and maintain the freedom of such persons, and will do no act or acts to repress such persons, or any of them, in any efforts they may make for their actual freedom.

That the Executive will, on the first day of January aforesaid, by proclamation, designate the States and parts of States, if any, in which the people thereof, respectively, shall then be in rebellion against the United States; and the fact that any State, or the people thereof, shall on that day be, in good faith, represented in the Congress of the United States by members chosen thereto at elections wherein a majority of the qualified voters of such State shall have participated, shall, in the absence of strong countervailing testimony, be deemed conclusive evidence that such State, and the people thereof, are not then in rebellion against the United States.

Now, therefore I, Abraham Lincoln, President of the United States, by virtue of the power in me vested as Commander-in-Chief, of the Army and Navy of the United States in time of actual armed rebellion against the authority and government of the United States, and as a fit and necessary war measure for suppressing said rebellion, do, on this first day of January, in the year of our Lord one thousand eight hundred and sixty-three, and in accordance with my purpose so to do publicly proclaimed for the full period of one hundred days, from the day first above mentioned, order and designate as the States and parts of States wherein the people thereof respectively, are this day in rebellion against the United States, the following, to wit:

Arkansas, Texas, Louisiana (except the Parishes of St. Bernard, Plaquemines, Jefferson, St. John, St. Charles, St. James Ascension, Assumption, Terrebonne, Lafourche, St. Mary, St. Martin, and Orleans, including the City of New Orleans), Mississippi, Alabama, Florida, Georgia, South Carolina, North Carolina, and Virginia, (except the forty-eight counties designated as West Virginia, and also the counties of Berkley, Accomac, Northampton, Elizabeth City, York, Princess Ann, and Norfolk, including the cities of Norfolk and Portsmouth), and which excepted parts, are for the present, left precisely as if this proclamation were not issued.

And by virtue of the power, and for the purpose aforesaid, I do order and declare that all persons held as slaves within said designated States, and parts of States, are, and henceforward shall be free; and that the Executive government of the United States, including the military and naval authorities thereof, will recognize and maintain the freedom of said persons.

And I hereby enjoin upon the people so declared to be free to abstain from all violence, unless in necessary self-defence; and I recommend to them that, in all cases when allowed, they labor faithfully for reasonable wages.

And I further declare and make known, that such persons of suitable condition, will be received into the armed service of the United States to garrison forts, positions, stations, and other places, and to man vessels of all sorts in said service.

And upon this act, sincerely believed to be an act of justice, warranted by the Constitution, upon military necessity, I invoke the considerate judgment of mankind, and the gracious favor of Almighty God.

In witness whereof, I have hereunto set my hand and caused the seal of the United States to be affixed.

Done at the City of Washington, this first day of January, in the year of our Lord one thousand eight hundred and sixty three, and of the Independence of the United States of America the eighty-seventh.

By the President: Abraham Lincoln
William H. Seward, Secretary of State

As Lincoln had hoped, the Proclamation turned foreign popular opinion in favor of the Union by adding the ending of slavery as a goal of the war. That shift ended the Confederacy's hopes of gaining official recognition, particularly from the UK, which had abolished slavery. The Proclamation also solidified Lincoln's support among the rapidly growing abolitionist element of the Republican Party and ensured they would not block his renomination in 1864.

In his famous Gettysburg Address in November 1863, Lincoln made indirect reference to the Proclamation and the ending of slavery as a war goal with the phrase "new birth of freedom."

As the Civil War ground to its last shuddering close in 1866, the freedom and equality of African Americans still had a long way to go. Many states began to immediately pass laws, now referred to as "Black Codes," aimed at limiting the civil rights and civil liberties of blacks by controlling the labor and movement of newly freed slaves.

These were followed by many state and local laws known infamously as the "Jim Crow" laws, which would last from 1876 all the way until the civil rights actions led to their end in 1965. They mandated *de jure* racial segregation in all public facilities in southern states of the former Confederacy, starting in 1890, with a "separate but equal" status for African Americans, and led to conditions for African Americans that tended to be inferior to those provided for white Americans.

And what became of those blacks who had fought on the side of the Union? After the Civil War, the regiments of black soldiers who had fought on behalf of the North, known as the United States Colored Troops, were reformed into two Cavalry troops, the 9th and 10th U.S. Cavalry. Eventually they formed two black infantry regiments, the 24th and 25th, which came to be known as the Buffalo Soldiers, a fearful honorific given them by the Native American Indians they were sent out West to fight. These soldiers distinguished themselves well, with thirteen enlisted men and six officers from the four regiments earning the Medal of Honor during the Indian Wars, and many serving in the Spanish-American War, where they won five more medals of honor.

Meanwhile, conditions in the South deteriorated for African Americans to the extent that many blacks began to migrate in great numbers from the South, many to the Midwest. Cities like Chicago doubled its black population every ten years in 1870, 1880, and 1890.

By 1881, the first Jim Crow laws segregating railroad coaches was passed by Tennessee, later by Florida, and then by Texas. Worse, in the decade from 1882 until 1892, the lynching of blacks increased, with more than 1,400 known instances.

Some African Americans already knew that the path upward would involve education. In 1881, the Tuskegee Institute, headed by Booker T. Washington, was founded. In 1895, Washington also attained national prominence for his Atlanta Address, which attracted the attention of politicians and the public, making him the representative of the last generation of black American leaders born in slavery and a popular spokesperson for African American citizens.

Each step was not always forward. In 1898, the literacy tests and poll taxes that were used to keep blacks from voting were upheld by the *Williams v. Mississippi* Supreme Court decision.

Nevertheless, efforts continued to be made to turn around the damage done by the reconstruction period of the South. In 1903, the General Education Board, which was endowed by John D. Rockefeller, supported better instruction for teachers of black schools in the South. In 1905, W.E.B. Du Bois founded the Niagara Movement and had a Niagara Conference to urge equal civil and economic rights, better education and justice for blacks, and an end to segregation. In 1909, the NAACP was formed. The National Urban League was also founded specifically to help blacks who were migrating to cities deal with social and economic issues. The 1920s to 1930s boomed with the Harlem Renaissance, a black cultural movement.

The country was still far from settled, though, in respect to accepting African Americans as equals. The Ku Klux Klan grew from an estimated one hundred thousand members in 27 states to an estimated four to four-and-a-half million members by 1924.

Steps Forward and Back

The tug-of-war of slow, halting progress continued, with seemingly as many steps backward as forward. In 1927, the Texas law that kept blacks from voting in Democratic elections was overturned by the Supreme Court (*Nixon v. Herndon*).

In 1935, the Harlem riots ended with three killed and as much as $2 million in damages. Considered an early race riot, Mayor LaGuardia ordered a multi-racial Mayor's Commission on Conditions in Harlem headed by African American sociologist E. Franklin Frazier to investigate the causes of the riot.

A bright spot in the Olympics of 1936 in Berlin came when Jesse Owens won four gold medals in track and field events and upset Hitler as a consequence.

Even brighter, on June 25, 1941, President Franklin D. Roosevelt issued Executive Order 8802, forbidding discrimination in employment in government and defense industries.

From 1941 to 1960, the black migration northward continued, with 43 cities outside the South doubling their black population.

The Congress of Racial Equality (CORE) was founded in 1942 by James Farmer.

Race riots erupted in Detroit, Michigan, and Mobile, Alabama, in 1943 over the employment of blacks.

On December 5, 1946, President Harry Truman issued Executive Order 9802 creating the Presidential Committee on Civil Rights. He followed that in 1948 with Executive Order 9981, which barred segregation in the armed forces and barred discrimination in federal civil service positions.

On July 12, 1951, rioting broke out in Cicero, Illinois, over segregated housing and grew so severe that the National Guard was called out.

In 1954, the Little Rock Crisis took center stage. On May 17, the U.S. Supreme Court ruled in *Brown v. Topeka Board of Education* that segregated schools are "inherently unequal." In September 1957, as a result of that ruling, nine African American students enrolled at Central High School in Little Rock, Arkansas. The ensuing, often violent, struggle between segregationists and integrationists, the State of Arkansas and the federal government, President Dwight D. Eisenhower and Arkansas Governor Orval Faubus, gained worldwide attention.

Thus, the time went by in the 100 years following the Emancipation Proclamation, with none of the freedom and equality promised fully delivered. The stage was set for someone to come to the front of the civil rights movement and lead, and that was about to happen.

FIGHTING FOR THE RIGHTS DUE ALL AMERICANS: THE ROAD TO THE MARCH

DR. MARTIN LUTHER KING, JR. first became enamored of the life and efforts of Mahatma Gandhi's nonviolent marches to achieve humane objectives through passive resistance when he was getting his divinity degree at Crozer Theological Seminary. He had already obtained a degree from Morehouse College at the age of 19 and would hold a Ph.D. from Boston University by 1955.

Born to parents who were by anyone's standards well off, he could have chosen a number of paths in life, yet he would take the one where he would be arrested, where crowds he led would be set on by police, dogs, and fire hoses, by jeers and rocks thrown by hostile mobs, and by bombs set in churches that even took the lives of children.

King's first encounter with a racial crisis happened in Montgomery, Alabama, where he was pastor of the Dexter Avenue Baptist Church. Tension had been mounting over the local transit company's policy of segregated public buses when civil rights activist Rosa Parks refused to give up her bus seat to a white man. Elected president of the Montgomery Improvement Association, which was organized to boycott the transit company, King's now famous initial stated principal was, "We will not resort to violence. We will not degrade ourselves with hatred. Love will be returned for hate." A one-day boycott turned into a much longer one when resistance in the form of intimidation, threats, mass arrests, and even physical violence only strengthened the resolve of the boycotters to stay nonviolent themselves.

The result came a year later when the Supreme Court ruled Alabama's segregated bus policy to be unconstitutional. People of all races rode the buses together, all from a well-organized, successful nonviolent effort.

A movie theater sign in Birmingham, a city that had a well-deserved reputation as the most segregated and racially violent city in the deep South. Its long string of unsolved racist bombings, many attributed to the KKK, earned the city the epithet Bombingham. 1963.

With that template in mind, King, along with Ralph Abernathy and other civil rights activists, organized the Southern Christian Leadership Conference (SCLC) in 1957. King served as the group's first president, and the SCLC moved from Montgomery, Alabama, to Atlanta, Georgia, when King became associate pastor of the Ebenezer Baptist Church.

Rosa Parks and her husband, Raymond, would both lose their jobs over the Montgomery bus incident but, when they moved to Detroit, Rosa remained an active worker for both the NAACP and the SCLC.

These were contentious times, with tension almost always beneath the surface. Awareness was ever growing, but the resistance to civil rights was often vigorous, even harsh. The times were defined by Ralph Ellison's *The Invisible Man*, published in 1952, that addressed many of the social and intellectual issues facing African Americans early in the twentieth century, how African Americans continued to be treated as a subculture that was nearly invisible to whites. The Voting Rights Act would be brought before Congress five times in the 1950s, only to be defeated each time by southern Democrats, led by Texans Sam Rayburn and Lyndon B. Johnson.

The tension and unrest continued to grow, yet Dr. Martin Luther King, Jr. stayed true to his intention to make change peacefully. In 1959 he published a short book called *The Measure of a Man*, which contained his sermons like, "What Is Man?" and "The Dimensions of a Complete Life." The sermons balanced an argument for man's need for God's love and criticized the racial injustices of Western civilization.

The King-encouraged peaceful approach led to the Freedom Riders, civil rights activists who rode interstate buses into the segregated southern United States from 1961 and later to challenge the nonenforcement of the U.S. Supreme Court decisions of *Irene Morgan v. Commonwealth of Virginia* (1946) and *Boyton v. Virginia* (1960), which ruled that segregated public buses were unconstitutional. The southern states had ignored the rulings, and the federal government had done nothing to enforce them. The first Freedom Ride left Washington, D.C., on May 4, 1961 and was scheduled to arrive in New Orleans on May 17.

In 1961, a desegregation coalition formed in Albany, Georgia, and became known as the Albany Movement. In December of that year, Martin Luther King, Jr. and the SCLC became involved. The movement mobilized thousands of citizens for a nonviolent confrontation on every aspect of segregation within the city and attracted nationwide attention. When King first visited on December 15, 1961, he had planned to stay a day or so and return home. The following day he got swept up in a mass arrest of peaceful demonstrators. To leverage the point being made, he declined bail until the city made concessions.

In April 1963, the SCLC began its campaign against racial segregation and economic injustice in Birmingham, Alabama. The campaign again used nonviolent but intentionally confrontational tactics, developed in part by Rev. Wyatt Tee Walker. Black people in Birmingham, along with members of the SCLC, occupied public spaces with marches and sit-ins, openly violating laws that they considered unjust.

During a mass meeting at the 16th Street Baptist Church, King urges his supporters to join the demonstrations. Birmingham, Alabama. 1963.

Not all that far away in Jackson, Mississippi, on June 12, 1963, a Mississippi desegregation leader, Medgar Evans, was killed by gunfire.

On June 11, 1963, John F. Kennedy called for a Civil Rights Act in his civil rights speech, in which he asked for legislation "giving all Americans the right to be served in facilities which are open to the public—hotels, restaurants, theaters, retail stores, and similar establishments," as well as "greater protection for the right to vote." Kennedy delivered this speech following a series of protests from the African American community, the most recent being the Birmingham campaign, which had concluded in May 1963.

Looking back, historically, these were small nonviolent successes, practice sessions for something far bigger and grander that was about to take place.

An eloquent speaker to his congregation at the 16th Street Baptist Church, King convinced many to help demonstrate. Birmingham, Alabama. 1963.

An enthusiastic response by the audience at the mass rally at the 16th Street
Baptist Church. Birmingham, Alabama. 1963.

King knew how to touch the hearts of his audience at the mass rally at the 16th Street Baptist Church. Birmingham, Alabama. 1963.

In the 16th Street Baptist Church, children crusaders link hands and sing, "We shall overcome" prior to the demonstration. Birmingham, Alabama. June 1963.

Concerned young people at the planning session for the Children's Crusade in the basement of the 16th Street Baptist Church. Birmingham, Alabama. June 1963.

Children's Crusade demonstrators leave 16th Street Baptist Church. Birmingham.
June 1963.

Young demonstrators of the Children's Crusade being arrested by the Birmingham police.
June 1963.

The Children's Crusade. The police had contained the demonstrations to the black part of town. But by filling the jails, the protestors immobilized the police—and the next wave of demonstrators could peacefully protest for the first time in downtown Birmingham. The jails were flooded, the city was paralyzed, and the white leadership realized it had to come to the bargaining table. 1963.

Arrested Children's Crusaders are placed on school buses as a massive number of demonstrators are sent off to be detained in the Birmingham Athletic Field. June 1963.

Improvised prisons: High school student demonstrators are detained in a sports stadium. Birmingham, Alabama. June 1963.

An arrest outside Loveman's Department Store. Birmingham, Alabama. June 1963.

An innocent bystander being arrested. Birmingham, Alabama. June 1963.

A picketer under arrest behind Loveman's department store. The protest focused on segregation and unfair hiring practices. Birmingham was a turning point. It was the first time the Movement took on such a large city. King called it the most segregated city in America. June 1963.

"Hell, no!" A downed onlooker during the hosings rises up enraged. Birmingham, Alabama. June 1963.

Demonstrators hold on to one another to face the full force of the fire hoses that peeled the bark off the trees in Kelly Ingram Park. Birmingham, Alabama. June 1963.

No man is an island. The police and firemen used a brute show of force to try to stop the ongoing demonstrations. It didn't work. Rather than fleeing, the protestors hung onto each other and were able to stand up to the full fury of the water, though not without casualties. As Dr. King later said, "I am startled that out of so much pain some beauty came." Kelly Ingram Park, Birmingham, Alabama. June 1963.

THE MARCH ITSELF

AUGUST 28, 1963

Photographs and Captions: Bob Adelman

THE TIME WAS RIGHT, 100 years after the signing of the Emancipation Proclamation.

The germ of the idea for the march was generated by A. Philip Randolph, the president of the Negro American Labor Council, vice president of the AFL-CIO, and the president of the Brotherhood of Sleeping Car Porters. He and Bayard Rustin, a pacifist and fellow civil rights activist, had planned a march like this before back in 1941. When the proposed numbers of those planning to attend the march in 1941 grew to as high as 100,000, President Franklin Roosevelt urged them to call off the demonstration. When they declined, Roosevelt issued Executive Order 8802, which became the First Employment Act, banning discrimination in federal jobs and defense industries. As a result of this action, the 1941 proposed march was called off.

Because of the growing civil rights movement, the 1963 march had far more steam and political clout behind it than the planned event of 1941. In addition to Randolph, who would head the march, there were Dr. Martin Luther King, Jr., president of the Southern Christian Leadership Conference; Roy Wilkins, president of the NAACP; John Lewis, chairman of the Student Nonviolent Coordinating Committee; James Farmer, president of the Congress of Racial Equality; and Whitney Young, president of the National Urban League.

Bayard Rustin, who had been with Randolph in planning the 1941 march, and who was good friends with Dr. Martin Luther King, Jr., became the march's deputy director and planner of logistics. Rustin put together and led the team of activists and organizers who publicized the march and recruited the marchers, provided the marshals, and set up the details of such a mass march in the nation's capital, one of the largest political rallies for human rights in United States history. He needed to coordinate more than 2,000 buses, 21 special trains, 10 chartered airliners, and uncounted cars converging on Washington on August 28, while all regularly scheduled planes, trains, and buses were also filled to capacity. It was one big march.

King was one that courted controversy, because he was one of the key figures who acceded to the wishes of President John F. Kennedy in changing the focus of the march. Kennedy initially opposed the march because he was concerned it would negatively impact the drive for passage of civil rights legislation. However, the organizers were firm that the march would proceed no matter what. With the march going forward, Kennedy decided it was important to work to ensure its success. Because Kennedy was concerned the turnout would be less than 100,000, he enlisted the aid of additional church leaders and the UAW union to help mobilize demonstrators for the cause.

The media turned out, too, for this march. Newspapers, radio, and the all-important television exposure from major networks even carried the speeches and offered commentaries. Hundreds of technicians and cameramen swarmed the area. Cameras were everywhere, even atop the Washington Monument—more cameras than had covered the recent presidential inauguration of John F. Kennedy.

The people turned out as well. The general consensus often puts the number of participants at a quarter of a million, whereas other estimates go as high as 300,000, with about 75%–80% of them black and the rest white and nonblack minorities.

A. Phillip Randolph, Martin Luther King, Jr., and James Farmer, all three civil rights leaders, meet at a private lunch to plan the March on Washington. New York City. Summer 1963.

Martin Luther King, Jr. exhorts parishioners to support the March on Washington. Brooklyn. Summer 1963.

King receives a check supporting the march from church officials in Brooklyn. He traveled 25 million miles in his life, much of it devoted to fundraising. Brooklyn. Summer 1963.

Demonstrators, mainly carried by buses, arrive in downtown Washington to assemble for the historic march. August 28, 1963.

A freedom walker, one of the demonstrators who walked to Washington, as many did from all parts of country, arrives at the demonstration. August 28, 1963.

Marchers assemble at the Washington Monument. August 28. 1963.

Stars were out as well, publicly supporting the call for civil and economic rights for African Americans. Mahalia Jackson, Bob Dylan, Joan Baez, Marian Anderson, Josh White, and Peter, Paul, and Mary gave musical performances. Harry Belafonte, Marlon Brando, Diahann Carroll, Ossie Davis, Sammy Davis Jr., Lena Horne, Paul Newman, and Charlton Heston were there, and Sidney Poitier read a speech written by James Baldwin.

Some of the demonstration participants, who came from the South, related incidents of being harassed on the way, but they made it. At the event itself, though, the swarms of police that had been called out to maintain peace became mere observers because the crowd, though large, was orderly and lived up to its intent to make a nonviolent demonstration.

Ossie Davis, the Master of Ceremony of the event, at the assembly point near the Washington Monument, holds up the official poster for the march. August 28, 1963.

Joan Baez entertains the crowd with her sonorous folk singing. August 28, 1963.

Odetta, Peter, Paul, and Mary, Joan Baez, and other performers sing for the crowd assembling at the base of the Washington Monument. August 28, 1963.

Bayard Rustin, organizer of the March on Washington, addresses the marchers assembling at the Washington Monument. August 28, 1963.

Rosa Parks. Washington, D.C. August 28, 1963.

Dorothy Height addresses the marchers assembling at the foot of the Washington Monument. Her pin describes the day as an "Emancipation March of Washington." August 28, 1963.

"When the SPIRIT says MOVE, you MOVE!" Marchers assembling at the Washington Monument, Washington, D.C. August 28, 1963.

Freedom walker. A demonstrator who marched from Clarksdale, Mississippi, to Washington, D.C., celebrates the protests near the Washington Monument. August 28, 1963.

Protestors assemble near Washington Monument with a coffin to bury Jim Crow. Washington, D.C., August 28, 1963.

Redemption: Protestor demands the promise of full equality promised in the Thirteenth, Fourteenth, and Fifteenth Amendments at the assembly at the Washington Monument. Washington, D.C. August 28, 1963.

Auto worker protestor assembles near the Washington Monument. August 28, 1963.

Although interracial marriage
was not on the program, this
father with his two children
has his own agenda. At the
time, many states had laws
prohibiting mixed marriages.
August 28, 1963.

Distaff members of the Interracial Marriage Club assemble at the beginning of the March. August 28, 1963.

Marchers begin to move toward the Lincoln Memorial. Washington, D.C.
August 28, 1963.

Assembled marchers begin the journey to the Lincoln Memorial. Washington, D.C. August 28, 1963.

Marchers pass the reflecting pool on their way to the Lincoln Memorial.
Washington, D.C. August 28, 1963.

Marchers en route to the Lincoln Memorial. Washington, D.C. 1963.

Marching alongside the reflecting pool, protestors head to the Lincoln Memorial with the Washington Monument and the Capital Dome in the background. Washington, D.C. August 28, 1963.

Mirrored in the reflecting pool, protestors head toward the Lincoln Memorial.
Washington, D.C. August 28, 1963.

Marchers from Newark, New Jersey, who came to the demonstration by bus, approach
the Lincoln Memorial. Washington, D.C. August 28, 1963.

Exuberant protestors approach the Lincoln Memorial. Washington, D.C. August 28, 1963.

Marchers protesting social and economic injustice approach the Lincoln Memorial. Washington, D.C. August 28, 1963.

Marchers walking along the mall passing federal buildings are almost to the Lincoln Memorial. Washington, D.C. August 28, 1963.

Protestors from all walks of life, many in their Sunday best, congregate on the mall leading to the Lincoln Memorial. Washington, D.C. August 28, 1963.

Proud marchers advance along the mall to the Lincoln Memorial. Washington, D.C. August 28, 1963.

Marchers on the mall pass federal buildings. Washington, D.C. August 28, 1963.

There were many speakers. In addition to the leaders of the six large organizing civil rights groups—James Farmer had to have his speech read by Floyd McKissik, because Farmer was imprisoned in Louisiana at the time—there were speeches from Catholic, Protestant, and Jewish religious leaders, as well as from labor leader Walter Reuther. Josephine Baker introduced Rosa Parks and several other "Negro Women Fighters for Freedom."

Ministers of various denominations march toward the Lincoln Memorial. Washington, D.C. August 28, 1963.

Determined protestors mass at the foot of the Lincoln Memorial. Washington, D.C. August 28, 1963.

Holding a handmade sign, a marcher approaches the end of the march. Washington, D.C. August 28, 1963.

So vast is the throng, the majority of marchers cannot advance past the perimeter of the reflecting pool. Washington, D.C. August 28, 1963.

Pressed up against one another, marchers reach their destination, the Lincoln Memorial. Washington, D.C. August 28, 1963.

Clarksdale, Mississippi, freedom walkers walked from Clarksdale to Washington, D.C. They proudly assemble, holding their demands up high. August 28, 1963.

High-spirited Movement members celebrate. The long-deferred promise of racial equality is now on the national agenda. Washington, D.C. August 28, 1963.

Marchers assembled at the Lincoln Memorial await the opening ceremonies.
Washington, D.C. August 28, 1963.

Patiently awaiting the opening ceremonies. Washington, D.C. August 28, 1963.

Invited guests are seated near the steps of the Lincoln Memorial. In this assemblage are actors Robert Ryan and Tony Franciosa, New York City Mayor Robert Wagner, writer James Baldwin, and many other dignitaries. Washington, D.C. August 28, 1963.

In a private moment, Norman Mailer cools off in the shade of a tree. Washington, D.C. August 28, 1963.

Two good Samaritans help a demonstrator suffering from the heat. Washington, D.C.
August 28, 1963.

Seated in front of the Lincoln Memorial, honored guests from all walks of life await the opening of the ceremony. Washington, D.C. August 28, 1963.

Honored guest Rosa Parks, heroine of the Movement, awaits the opening remarks. Washington, D.C. August 28, 1963.

Members of the Congressional Delegation greet the assembled crowd. Standing in the front row is Jacob Javits. Next to him in a white suit is Congressman Adam Clayton Powell. The purpose of the demonstration is to demand that Congress pass pending legislation outlawing state-supported segregation in public places throughout the land. Washington, D.C. August 28, 1963.

Leaders, including (from left to right) National Urban League Director Whitney Young, Jr., the Reverend Ralph Abernathy, and Walter Reuther, head of the CIO, join King to pledge allegiance at the beginning of the ceremony at the Lincoln Memorial. Washington, D.C. August 28, 1963.

The ceremony begins with the singing of the National Anthem. Washington, D.C. August 28, 1963.

Mahalia Jackson, greatest gospel singer of her time, moves the crowd of 250,000 people at the march. Washington, D.C. August 28, 1963.

A. Phillip Randolph, director of the March on Washington, gives the opening remarks. Since 1941, it was Randolph's idea that a massive march to protest the unfair treatment of African Americans should come to Washington. The memorial's text is in the background. Washington, D.C. August 28, 1963.

An attentive crowd listens intently as the speeches begin. Washington, D.C. August 28, 1963.

Reverend Fred Shuttlesworth, leader of the protest in Birmingham, addresses the marchers atop the steps of the Lincoln Memorial. He is seen through a military honor guard. Washington, D.C. August 28, 1963.

In national director James Farmer's absence, Floyd McKissick, chairman of CORE, addresses the march. Mrs. King and Dr. King are on the podium. Washington, D.C. August 28, 1963.

John Lewis, chairman of SNCC, rises to address the march. All of 22 at the time, he had just returned from having his militant speech severely edited and toned down by his fellow speakers and march organizers.

Seated on the podium, CORE chairman Floyd McKissick listens to speeches made by his fellow civil rights leaders.

In coveralls, Rudy Lombard, vice chairman of CORE, with legendary freedom rider James Peck.

A thoughtful guest listens to the speeches.

Marlon Brando, an honored guest, is interviewed on the steps of the Lincoln Memorial at the final ceremonies of the March on Washington. 1963.

Reverend Wyatt T. Walker, key aide of Dr. King (left), and Reverend Fred Shuttlesworth, leader of the Birmingham protests, are delighted by the massive turnout.

Harry Belafonte, actor, singer, and social activist, chats with Burt Lancaster at the side of the Lincoln Memorial.

Marlon Brando, Burt Lancaster, Harry Belafonte, and Charlton Heston on the steps of the Lincoln Memorial during the ceremonies.

Marlon Brando, Burt Lancaster, Harry Bellafonte, and Charlton Heston discuss the issues.

Sammy Davis Jr. talks with Harry Belafonte on the steps of the Lincoln Memorial at the culmination of the March on Washington.

Reverend Fred Shuttlesworth enjoying the ceremony at the March on Washington.

Leon Bibb, a Louisville folk singer who appeared on *The Ed Sullivan Show*, Broadway, and the Newport Jazz Festival, was later blacklisted along with people like Paul Robeson for ties to left-wing groups and causes. He listens to the proceedings on the steps of the Lincoln Memorial.

James Baldwin, sitting near heroic freedom rider Jerome Smith, listens to speakers at the ceremony in front of the Lincoln Memorial. March on Washington. 1963.

"Amen, brother!" Enthusiastic march participants stir as King begins to speak. Washington, D.C. 1963.

A speech by John Lewis, who represented the Student Nonviolent Coordinating Committee, was circulated early. There were several suggested cuts to tone it down and keep it in tune with the passive resistance theme. Among those cuts were Lewis calling Kennedy's civil rights bill "too little, too late," asking "which side is the federal government on?", and declaring that they would march "through the Heart of Dixie, the way Sherman did" and "burn Jim Crow to the ground—nonviolently."

But the speech that stole the show, garnered the most media coverage, and is venerated to this day happened on the steps of the Lincoln Memorial when Rev. Martin Luther King, Jr. spoke to the crowd and Mahalia Jackson called out to him from the crowd for him to "Tell them about the dream." He diverted from his planned speech and did just that. He told them about the dream.

Martin Luther King, Jr. begins his historic "I Have a Dream" speech, reading at first from his prepared texts.

The Full Text of the "I Have a Dream" Speech

By The Rev. Martin Luther King, Jr.,
August 28, 1963

I am happy to join with you today in what will go down in history as the greatest demonstration for freedom in the history of our nation.

Five score years ago, a great American, in whose symbolic shadow we stand, signed the Emancipation Proclamation. This momentous decree came as a great beacon light of hope to millions of Negro slaves who had been seared in the flames of withering injustice. It came as a joyous day-break to end the long night of captivity.

But one hundred years later, we must face the tragic fact that the Negro is still not free. One hundred years later, the life of the Negro is still sadly crippled by the manacles of segregation and the chains of discrimination. One hundred years later, the Negro lives on a lonely island of poverty in the midst of a vast ocean of material prosperity. One hundred years later, the Negro is still languishing in the corners of American society and finds himself an exile in his own land. So we have come here today to dramatize an appalling condition.

In a sense we have come to our nation's capital to cash a check. When the architects of our republic wrote the magnificent words of the Constitution and the Declaration of Independence, they were signing a promissory note to which every American was to fall heir. This note was a promise that all men would be guaranteed the inalienable rights of life, liberty, and the pur-suit of happiness.

It is obvious today that America has defaulted on this promissory note inso-far as her citizens of color are concerned. Instead of honoring this sacred obligation, America has given the Negro people a bad check, which has come back marked "insufficient funds." But we refuse to believe that the bank of justice is bankrupt. We refuse to believe that there are insufficient funds in the great vaults of opportunity of this nation. So we have come to cash this check—a check that will give us upon demand the riches of freedom and the security of justice. We have also come to this hallowed spot to remind America of the fierce urgency of now. This is no time to engage in the luxury of cooling off or to take the tranquilizing drug of gradualism. Now is the time to rise from the dark and desolate valley of segregation to the sunlit path of racial justice. Now is the time to open the doors of opportunity to all of God's children. Now is the time to lift our nation from the quicksands of racial injustice to the solid rock of brotherhood.

It would be fatal for the nation to overlook the urgency of the moment and to underestimate the determination of the Negro. This sweltering summer of the Negro's legitimate discontent will not pass until there is an invigorating autumn of freedom and equality. Nineteen sixty-three is not an end, but a beginning. Those who hope that the Negro needed to blow off steam and will now be content will have a rude awakening if the nation returns to business as usual. There will be neither rest nor tranquility in America until the Negro is granted his citizenship rights. The whirlwinds of revolt will continue to shake the foundations of our nation until the bright day of justice emerges.

But there is something that I must say to my people who stand on the warm threshold which leads into the palace of justice. In the process of gaining our rightful place we must not be guilty of wrongful deeds. Let us not seek to satisfy our thirst for freedom by drinking from the cup of bitterness and hatred.

We must forever conduct our struggle on the high plane of dignity and discipline. We must not allow our creative protest to degenerate into physical violence. Again and again we must rise to the majestic heights of meeting physical force with soul force. The marvelous new militancy which has engulfed the Negro community must not lead us to distrust of all white people, for many of our white brothers, as evidenced by their presence here today, have come to realize that their destiny is tied up with our destiny and their freedom is inextricably bound to our freedom. We cannot walk alone.

And as we walk, we must make the pledge that we shall march ahead. We cannot turn back. There are those who are asking the devotees of civil rights, "When will you be satisfied?" We can never be satisfied as long as our bodies, heavy with the fatigue of travel, cannot gain lodging in the motels of the highways and the hotels of the cities. We cannot be satisfied as long as the Negro's basic mobility is from a smaller ghetto to a larger one. We can never be satisfied as long as a Negro in Mississippi cannot vote and a Negro in New York believes he has nothing for which to vote. No, no, we are not satisfied, and we will not be satisfied until justice rolls down like waters and righteousness like a mighty stream.

I am not unmindful that some of you have come here out of great trials and tribulations. Some of you have come fresh from narrow cells. Some of you have come from areas where your quest for freedom left you battered by the storms of persecution and staggered by the winds of police brutality. You have been the veterans of creative suffering. Continue to work with the faith that unearned suffering is redemptive.

Go back to Mississippi, go back to Alabama, go back to Georgia, go back to Louisiana, go back to the slums and ghettos of our northern cities, knowing that somehow this situation can and will be changed. Let us not wallow in the valley of despair.

I say to you today, my friends, that in spite of the difficulties and frustrations of the moment, I still have a dream. It is a dream deeply rooted in the American dream.

I have a dream that one day this nation will rise up and live out the true meaning of its creed: "We hold these truths to be self-evident: that all men are created equal."

I have a dream that one day on the red hills of Georgia the sons of former slaves and the sons of former slave owners will be able to sit down together at a table of brotherhood.

I have a dream that one day even the state of Mississippi, a desert state, sweltering with the heat of injustice and oppression, will be transformed into an oasis of freedom and justice.

I have a dream that my four children will one day live in a nation where they will not be judged by the color of their skin but by the content of their character.

I have a dream today.

I have a dream that one day the state of Alabama, whose governor's lips are presently dripping with the words of interposition and nullification, will be transformed into a situation where little black boys and black girls will be able to join hands with little white boys and white girls and walk together as sisters and brothers.

I have a dream today.

I have a dream that one day every valley shall be exalted, every hill and mountain shall be made low, the rough places will be made plain, and the crooked places will be made straight, and the glory of the Lord shall be revealed, and all flesh shall see it together.

This is our hope. This is the faith with which I return to the South. With this faith we will be able to hew out of the mountain of despair a stone of hope. With this faith we will be able to transform the jangling discords of our nation into a beautiful symphony of brotherhood. With this faith we will be able to work together, to pray together, to struggle together, to go to jail together, to stand up for freedom together, knowing that we will be free one day.

This will be the day when all of God's children will be able to sing with a new meaning, "My country, 'tis of thee, sweet land of liberty, of thee I sing. Land where my fathers died, land of the pilgrim's pride, from every mountainside, let freedom ring."

And if America is to be a great nation this must become true. So let freedom ring from the prodigious hilltops of New Hampshire. Let freedom ring from the mighty mountains of New York. Let freedom ring from the heightening Alleghenies of Pennsylvania!

Let freedom ring from the snowcapped Rockies of Colorado!

Let freedom ring from the curvaceous slopes of California!

But not only that; let freedom ring from Stone Mountain of Georgia!

Let freedom ring from Lookout Mountain of Tennessee!

Let freedom ring from every hill and molehill of Mississippi. From every mountainside, let freedom ring.

And when this happens, when we allow freedom to ring, when we let it ring from every village and every hamlet, from every state and every city, we will be able to speed up that day when all of God's children, black men and white men, Jews and Gentiles, Protestants and Catholics, will be able to join hands and sing in the words of the old Negro spiritual, "Free at last! Free at last! Thank God Almighty, we are free at last!"

Listeners hear Martin Luther King, Jr.'s opening remarks.

An honor guard stands at attention as King speaks.

Audience members concentrate intently as King speaks. Washington, D.C. August 28, 1963.

King pauses in his historic address.

Still reading from his prepared speech, King waits during the enthusiastic response.

In coveralls, Jerome Smith, heroic freedom rider, reacts to King's speech.

Casting aside his prepared remarks, King extemporaneously begins to share his unforgettable message. Washington, D.C. 1963.

The Dreamer dreams. King continues to deliver his "I Have a Dream" speech. Washington, D.C. 1963.

The rapt audience hears King speak of the "true meaning of our destiny."
Washington, D.C. 1963.

King emotes, "It is obvious today that America has defaulted on this promissory note insofar as her citizens of color are concerned." Washington, D.C. 1963.

King speaks to a rising crescendo of applause. Washington, D.C. 1963.

King says, "Now is the time to rise from the dark and desolate valley of segregation to the sunlit path of racial justice." Washington, D.C. 1963.

The marchers listen intently as King shares their most fervent hopes. Washington, D.C. 1963.

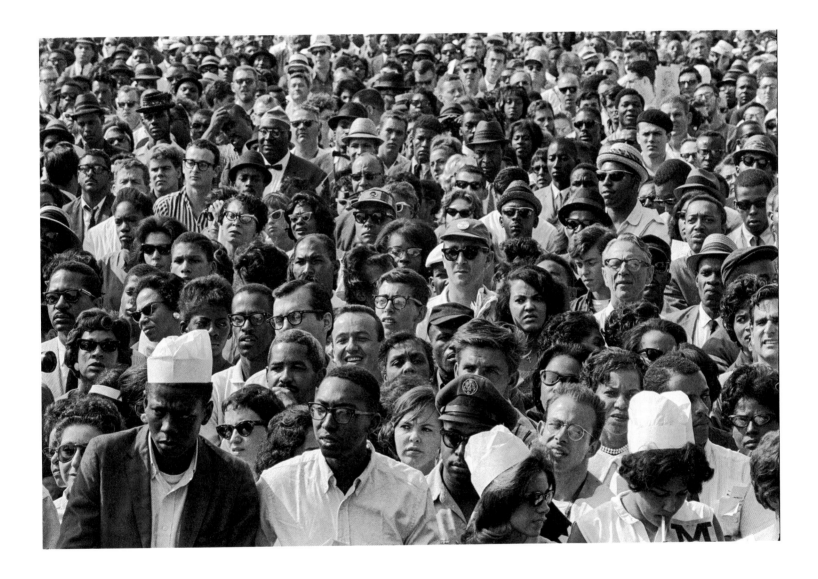

To mounting applause, King speaks, "We must forever conduct our struggle on the high plane of dignity and discipline." Washington, D.C. 1963.

King speaks, "I have a dream that one day this nation will rise up and live out the true meaning of its creed: We hold these truths to be self-evident: that all men are created equal." Washington, D.C. 1963.

Crowd reacts to King's imperishable words. Washington, D.C. 1963.

King shouts, "Let freedom ring from every hill and molehill of Mississippi. From every mountainside, let freedom ring!" Washington, D.C. 1963.

Crowd cheers wildly to the culmination of King's historic speech. Washington, D.C. 1963.

King ends his speech with the words of the old Negro spiritual, "Free at last! Free at last! Thank God Almighty, we are free at last!" Washington, D.C. 1963.

THE AFTERMATH: 1963–APRIL 4, 1968

THE MARCH ON WASHINGTON of 1963 was followed by more years of racial strife. Yet a strong seed had been sown of affirmation, of hope, of belief in the democratic process, and of faith in the capacity of blacks and whites to work together for racial equality.

The Civil Rights Act

One momentous event that followed the march and benefited the civil rights movement was the Civil Rights Act that was enacted on July 2, 1964. It outlawed major forms of discrimination against racial, ethnic, national, and religious minorities, and women. The bill had been earlier called for by the now-late President John F. Kennedy in his June 11, 1963 civil rights speech but was signed into law by Lyndon B. Johnson, who had once opposed voting rights for African Americans. Many credit the public demonstration of the march with making it clear that the tide had turned. The Act made it through Congress in spite of a 54-hour filibuster by southern congressmen from both parties. The opposition came from such congressmen as Strom Thurmond, Evert Dirksen, and Hubert Humphrey.

Lyndon B. Johnson, once an opponent but a consummate politician and now someone who could sense the change in the nation, told the legislators, "No memorial oration or eulogy could more eloquently honor President Kennedy's memory than the earliest possible passage of the civil rights bill for which he fought so long."

For the Southern Christian Leadership Conference (SCLC), it was a step forward but also the beginning of a long campaign to continue to strive for civil rights for African Americans. In 1964, King and the SCLC were the driving forces behind intense demonstrations in St. Augustine, Florida. The movement marched nightly through the city and experienced violent attacks from white supremacists. Hundreds of the marchers were arrested and jailed.

These efforts did not go unnoticed. On October 14, 1964, Martin Luther King, Jr. received the Nobel Peace Prize for combating racial inequality through nonviolence.

In December 1964, King and the SCLC joined forces with the Student Nonviolent Coordinating Committee (SNCC) in Selma, Alabama, where the SNCC had been working on voter registration for several months. A local judge issued an injunction that barred any gathering of three or more people affiliated with the SNCC, SCLC, DCVL, or any of 41 named civil rights leaders. This injunction temporarily halted civil rights activity until King openly defied it by speaking at Brown Chapel on January 2, 1965.

Next came the Selma to Montgomery marches. On March 7, 1965, King, James Bevel, and the SCLC, again in partial collaboration with the SNCC, attempted to organize a march from Selma, Alabama, to the state capital of Montgomery. The first attempt to march on that Sunday in March was aborted because of mob and police violence against the demonstrators. Six hundred marchers had assembled and planned to cross the Edmund Pettus Bridge over the Alabama River en route to Montgomery. Just short of the bridge, they found their way blocked by Alabama State Troopers and local police, who ordered them to turn around. When the protestors refused, the officers shot teargas and waded into the crowd, beating the nonviolent protestors with billy clubs. More than fifty of the peaceful demonstrators had to be hospitalized. This day has since become known as Bloody Sunday.

Bloody Sunday was a major turning point in the effort to gain public support for the civil rights movement, the clearest demonstration up to that time of the dramatic potential of King's nonviolence strategy. King, however, was not present.

King had met with officials in the Johnson administration on March 5 to request an injunction against any prosecution of the demonstrators. He did not attend the march due to church duties, but he later wrote, "If I had any idea that the state troopers would use the kind of brutality they did, I would have felt compelled to give up my church duties altogether to lead the line." Footage of police brutality against the protestors was broadcast extensively and aroused national public outrage.

King next attempted to organize a march for March 9. The SCLC petitioned for an injunction in federal court against the State of Alabama, which was denied. The judge issued an order blocking the march until after a hearing. Nonetheless, King led marchers on March 9 to the Edmund Pettus Bridge in Selma. Then he held a short prayer session before turning the marchers around and asking them to disperse so as not to violate the court order. The unexpected ending of this second march aroused the surprise and anger of many within the local movement. The march finally went ahead fully on March 25, 1965. At the conclusion of the march on the steps of the state capital, King delivered a speech that became known as "How Long, Not Long." In it, King stated that equal rights for African Americans could not be far away, "because the arc of the moral universe is long, but it bends toward justice."

The Voting Rights Act

On August 6, 1965, President Lyndon B. Johnson signed the Voting Rights Act into law. In the Oval Office watching him sign were Martin Luther King, Jr., Rosa Parks, and other civil rights leaders. This was another big step many feel could not have happened without the march.

The Voting Rights Act outlawed the sort of discriminatory practices, such as the literacy tests used in southern states, that had kept many African Americans from voting.

The Act was sent to Congress by President Johnson on March 17, 1965. The bill passed the Senate on May 26, 1965. The House was slower to give its approval. After five weeks of debate, it was finally passed on July 9. After differences between the two bills were resolved in conference, the House passed the Conference Report on August 3 and the Senate followed on August 4. On August 6, President Johnson signed the Act into law.

By 1965, concerted efforts to break the grip of state unequal treatment of minorities had been under way for some time but had achieved only modest success overall and in some areas had proved almost entirely ineffectual. The murder of voting-rights activists in Philadelphia, Missouri, gained national attention, along with numerous other acts of violence and terrorism.

It was that unprovoked attack by state troopers on peaceful marchers crossing the Edmund Pettus Bridge in Selma, Alabama, on their way to the state capitol in Montgomery, that persuaded the president and Congress to overcome southern legislators' resistance to effective voting rights legislation.

Congress determined that the existing federal anti-discrimination laws were insufficient to overcome the resistance by state officials to enforcement of the Fifteenth Amendment. The legislative hearings showed that the Department of Justice's efforts to eliminate discriminatory election practices by litigation on a case-by-case basis had been unsuccessful in opening the registration process; as soon as one discriminatory practice or procedure was proven to be unconstitutional and enjoined, a new one would be substituted in its place and litigation would have to commence anew.

Soon after passage of the Voting Rights Act, federal examiners were conducting voter registration checks and found that black voter registration had begun a sharp increase. The cumulative effect of the Supreme Court's decisions, Congress's enactment of voting rights legislation, and the ongoing efforts of concerned private citizens and the Department of Justice had been to restore the right to vote guaranteed by the Fourteenth and Fifteenth Amendments.

The Voting Rights Act itself has been called the single most effective piece of civil rights legislation ever passed by Congress.[4]

Ongoing SCLC Activities

When the Meredith, Mississippi, "March Against Fear" passed through Grenada, Mississippi, on June 15, 1966, it sparked months of civil rights activity on the part of Grenada blacks. They formed the Grenada County Freedom Movement (GCFM) as an SCLC affiliate, and within days they had 1,300 blacks registered to vote.

Although the Civil Rights Act of 1964 had outlawed segregation of public facilities, the law had not been applied in Grenada, which still maintained rigid segregation. After black students were arrested for trying to sit downstairs in the "white" section of the movie theater, the SCLC and the GCFM demanded that all forms of segregation be eliminated. They called for a boycott of white merchants. Over the summer, the number of protests increased, and many demonstrators and SCLC organizers were arrested as police enforced the old Jim Crow social order. In July and August, large mobs of white segregationists mobilized by the KKK violently attacked peaceful marchers and news reporters with rocks, bottles, baseball bats, and steel pipes.

When the new school year began in September, the SCLC and the GCFM encouraged more than 450 black students to register at the formerly white schools under a court desegregation order. This was by far the largest school integration attempt in Mississippi since the *Brown v. Board of Education* ruling in 1954. The all-white school board of Grenada County resisted fiercely. Whites threatened black parents with economic retaliation if they did not withdraw their children, and by the first day of school the number of black children registered in the white schools had dropped to approximately 250. On the first day of class, September 12, a furious white mob organized by the KKK attacked the black children and their parents with clubs, chains, whips, and pipes as they walked to school, injuring many and hospitalizing several with broken bones. Police and Mississippi State Troopers made no effort to halt or deter the mob violence.

Over the following days, white mobs continued to attack the black children until public pressure and a federal court order finally forced Mississippi lawmen to intervene. By the end of the first week, many black parents had withdrawn their children from the white schools out of fear for their safety, but approximately 150 black students continued to attend, the largest school integration in state history at that point in time.

Inside the schools, blacks were harassed by white teachers, threatened and attacked by white students, and expelled on flimsy pretexts by school officials. By mid-October, the number of blacks attending the white schools had dropped to roughly 70. When school officials refused to meet with a delegation of black parents, black students began boycotting both the white and the black schools in protest. Many children, parents, GCFM activists, and SCLC organizers were arrested for protesting the school situation. By the end of October, almost all of the 2,600 black students in Grenada County were boycotting school. The boycott did not end until early November when

SCLC attorneys were granted a federal court order that the school system must treat everyone equal regardless of race and meet with black parents.

After several successes in the South, King and others in the civil rights organizations sought to spread the movement to the North later in 1966. King and Ralph Abernathy, both from the middle class, moved into a building at 1550 South Hamlin Avenue, in the slums of North Lawndale on the west side of Chicago, as an educational experience and to demonstrate their support and empathy for the poor.

The SCLC formed a coalition with the Coordinating Council of Community Organizations (CCCO), an organization founded by Albert Raby. The combined organizations' efforts were supported by The Chicago Freedom Movement. During that spring, several tests of real estate offices revealed racial steering: the discriminatory processing of housing requests made by couples who were exact matches in income, background, number of children, and other attributes where white couples were favored over black couples. Several larger marches were planned and executed in Bogan, Belmont Cragin, Jefferson Park, Evergreen Park (a suburb southwest of Chicago), Gage Park, and Marquette Park.

Abernathy said that the movement received a worse reception in Chicago than in the South. Marches, especially the one through Marquette Park on August 5, 1966, were met by bottles thrown by screaming throngs. Rioting seemed very possible. King, as always, remained opposed to staging a violent event, or one that could become violent. He negotiated an agreement with Mayor Richard J. Daly to cancel one march to avoid the violence that he feared would result. King was hit by a brick during another march yet continued to lead marches in the face of personal danger.

When King and his supporters returned to the South, they left Jesse Jackson, a seminary student who had previously joined the movement in the South, in charge of their organization. Jackson continued their struggle for civil rights by organizing the Operation Breadbasket movement that targeted chain stores that did not deal fairly with blacks.

In an April 4, 1967 appearance at the New York City Riverside Church—exactly one year before his death—King delivered a speech entitled "Beyond Vietnam." He spoke against the U.S. role in the war, arguing that the United States was in Vietnam "to occupy it as an American colony." He called the U.S. government "the greatest purveyor of violence in the world today." King also opposed the Vietnam War because it took money and resources that could have been spent on social welfare at home. Congress was spending more and more on the military and less and less on antipoverty programs.

Eldridge Cleaver's post-prison book *Soul on Ice* was published in 1968. A central premise of the book was the trouble of identification as a black soul that has been "colonized" by an oppressive white society.

In 1968, King and the SCLC organized the "Poor People's Campaign" to continue to address issues of economic justice. King traveled the country to assemble "a multiracial army of the poor" that would march on Washington to engage in nonviolent civil disobedience at the Capitol until Congress created an "economic bill of rights" for poor Americans. The campaign culminated in a march on Washington, D.C., demanding economic aid to the poorest communities of the United States.

King and the SCLC called on the government to invest in rebuilding America's cities. He felt that Congress had shown "hostility to the poor" by spending "military funds with alacrity and generosity." He contrasted this with the situation faced by poor Americans, claiming that Congress had merely provided "poverty funds with miserliness." His vision was for change that was more revolutionary than mere reform: he cited systematic flaws of "racism, poverty, militarism, and materialism," and argued that "reconstruction of society itself is the real issue to be faced."

The Poor People's Campaign was controversial even within the civil rights movement. Bayard Rustin resigned from it stating that the goals of the campaign were too broad and the demands unrealizable. He thought that these campaigns would accelerate the backlash and repression on the poor and the black.

The Day the King Fell

On April 4, 1968 at 6:01 p.m. a shot rang out as Martin Luther King, Jr. stood on the Lorraine Motel's second-floor balcony in Memphis. He was pronounced dead at St. Joseph's Hospital. Two months after King's death, escaped convict James Earl Ray was captured at London's Heathrow Airport while trying to leave the United Kingdom on a false Canadian passport in the name of Ramon George Sneyd, on his way to white-ruled Rhodesia. Ray was quickly extradited to Tennessee and charged with King's murder. He confessed to the assassination on March 10, 1969, although he recanted this confession three days later.

The plan to set up a shantytown in Washington, D.C., was carried out on May 2, 1968, soon after the April 4 assassination. Criticism of King's plan was subdued in the wake of his death, and the SCLC received an unprecedented wave of donations for the purpose of carrying it out. The campaign officially began in Memphis, on May 2, at the Lorraine Motel where King was murdered. Thousands of demonstrators arrived on the National Mall and established a camp they called "Resurrection City." They stayed for six weeks.

On October 16, 1968, at the Olympics in Mexico City, African American track and field athletes Tommie Smith and John Carlos, who had won gold and silver medals in the 200-meter race, raised black-gloved fists into the air and held them there during the length of the "Star Spangled Banner." Smith later said the gesture was not intended as a black power salute but as a human rights salute. The two athletes were expelled from the games.

Although the steps were small, they were sure. The efforts of King, the march, and the SCLC and other organizations increasing pressure for civil rights began to have a measurable effect. For one, in the November 5, 1968 presidential election, 51.4% of registered nonwhites voted, as compared to 44% in 1964, and black registration for voting in 11 southern states rose from 1,463,000 in 1960 to 3,449,000 in 1971. In the years from 1970 to 1973, the black migration that had been trending South to North reversed, and African Americans began moving from the North back to the South, reflecting economic factors.

The SCLC Through the Years That Lay Ahead

Through the years that followed, the SCLC pressed on with its efforts. Following Dr. Martin Luther King, Jr.'s first presidency from 1957–1968, Ralph Abernathy served as president from 1968–1977, Joseph Lowery from 1977–1997, Martin Luther King, III, from 1997–2004, Fred Shuttlesworth in 2004, Charles Kenzie Steele, Jr. from 2004–2009, and Howard W. Creecy, Jr. from 2009–2011. Isaac Newton Farris, Jr. has been serving as president since 2011.

Among the many distinguished members of the SCLC have been Ralph Abernathy, Maya Angelou, Ella Baker, James Bevel, Septima Clark, Dorothy Cotton, Walter E. Fauntroy, Curtis W. Harris, Jesse Jackson, Martin Luther King, III, Joseph Lowery, Diane Nash, James Orange, Fred Shuttlesworth, Charles Kenzie Steele, C.T. Vivian, Hosea Williams, Andrew Young, and Claud Young.

FIFTY YEARS LATER:
A LOOK AT TODAY

By Dr. Rodney Sampson

If Dr. Martin Luther King, Jr. had been asked if he believed America would elect a black president in 2008, he might not have answered yes. Then again, his dream was a very powerful one. He might have seen that as possible.

Could this have happened without the effects of the Civil Rights Act and Voting Rights Act being felt? Unlikely.

In spite of clear gains through the years, there is still a long ways to go and much for the Southern Christian Leadership Conference (SCLC) to help accomplish. Consider the state of America for African Americans 50 years after the march.

According to the U.S. Labor Department, the unemployment for African Americans fell substantially in January of 2013 to 13.6%. It remains significantly higher than the 8.5% rate of November 2007, just prior to the recession. Aggregate numbers showed that the African American community as a whole had exhibited poorer labor market outcomes than other races even prior to the recession and during the recovery, demonstrating that they often face different and greater challenges.[5]

It is not just the employment rate that presents a stark difference; the wealth gap between blacks and whites in America has risen to record highs. The median wealth of white households is 20 times that of black households and 18 times that of Hispanic households, according to a Pew Research Center analysis of newly available government data from 2009.[6]

In her book *The American Non-Dilemma: Racial Inequality Without Racism*,[7] Rutgers professor Nancy DiTomaso argues that whites use family, friends, and acquaintances to get as many as 70% of their jobs, a practice that continues to put African Americans at a disadvantage.

In their book *Documenting Desegregation: Racial and Gender Segregation in Private-Sector Employment Since the Civil Rights Act*,[8] Kevin Stainback and Donald Tomaskovic Devey make a compelling case for African Americans making no progress at all for equal opportunities in private firms since the 1980s—that the gains of the 1960s and 1970s have been cancelled out by resegregation in the job market.

Voting rights and conditions may have improved by large strides, but there is a long road to go before anyone can rest.

It would appear that the need for the SCLC is not over and that there is much left to do.

With new and needed goals to accomplish, this is why the SCLC takes this occasion to

- Celebrate the fiftieth anniversary of Dr. Martin Luther King's March on Washington for Jobs and Freedom.

- Celebrate the one-hundred fiftieth anniversary of President Abraham Lincoln's Emancipation of Southern Slaves.

- Celebrate men, women, causes, and companies that have demonstrated their commitment to the global cause of human, civil, and economic dignity.

- Relaunch Dr. King's last cause, the Poor People's Campaign, in the form of a Washington, D.C.–based SCLC Poverty Institute designed to address modern-day poverty and the wealth gap in America and beyond with definitive education, innovation, entrepreneurship, and investment-based collaborative programs.

The SCLC Poverty Institute, in collaboration with Opportunity Community Development Corporation and Kingonomics, intends to embrace this and the following causes:

- Research and publish findings in collaboration with top academic and research-based institutions. Identify definitive challenges and discover viable and achievable solutions to address the wealth gap among underserved and underrepresented communities in America and beyond.

- Advocate for federal, state, and local policy and legislation that decreases the wealth gap among minority and underserved communities in America and beyond.

- Facilitate exposure to youth, young adults, corporate executives, veterans, and the unemployed to the innovative industries and opportunities of the future.

- Provide economic, entrepreneurship, and investor-based education via Kingonomics conferences, boot camps, webinars, coaching, and mentorship.

- Facilitate the development of Opportunity Incubator Hubs in collaboration with entrepreneurial companies and investors with the definitive purpose of launching and accelerating start-up companies designed to service these industries' quest for innovation and efficiency.

- Develop collaborative partnerships with funding platforms designed to provide start-ups and growth stage companies with access to capital while simultaneously creating a global ecosystem of entrepreneurs and investors.

In the spirit of Dr. Martin Luther King, Jr., the SCLC and other civil rights organizations can say, "Our work is not done. We have a dream."

TIMELINE OF EVENTS

1814 — In the Treaty of Ghent that ended the War of 1812 between the United States and England on December 24, both the U.S. and British governments agreed to use their best efforts to abolish the international slave trade. England abolished slavery in 1833. The United States did not hold up to its end of the agreement.

1850 — Fugitive Slave Act required individuals to return runaway slaves to their owners.

1850–1860 — Underground railroad reached its peak.

1857 — Dred Scott Decision raised the issue of the status of slaves who had been held captive while residing in a free state.

1859 — Harper's Ferry: October 16, the radical abolitionist John Brown led a group of 21 men in a raid on the arsenal. Brown hoped to use the captured weapons to initiate a slave uprising throughout the South.

1862 — In January, Thaddeus Stevens, the Republican leader in the House of Representatives, called for total war against the rebellion to include emancipation of slaves, arguing that emancipation, by forcing the loss of enslaved labor, would ruin the rebel economy.

1862 — In July, Lincoln first discussed the proclamation with his Cabinet. He believed he needed a Union victory on the battlefield so his decision would appear positive and strong.

1862 — On September 22, the Battle of Antietam, in which Union troops turned back a Confederate invasion of Maryland, gave Lincoln his opportunity. Five days after Antietam, Lincoln called his Cabinet into session and issued the Preliminary Proclamation.

1862 — In July, Congress passed and Lincoln signed the Second Confiscation Act, containing provisions intended to liberate slaves held by "rebels."

1863 — On January 1, President Lincoln issued the Emancipation Proclamation.

1863 — In November, Lincoln's Gettysburg Address made indirect reference to the Proclamation and the ending of slavery as a war goal with the phrase "new birth of freedom."

Exempted states Maryland, Missouri, Tennessee, and West Virginia prohibited slavery by the end of the war.

Reconstruction plans were adopted in Arkansas and Tennessee.

1864 — Reconstruction abolished slavery in Louisiana.

1865 — On December 18, slavery remained legal in Delaware and Kentucky until the Thirteenth Amendment went into effect.

1866–1890s — After the Civil War, the regiments of black soldiers who had fought on behalf of the North, known as the United States Colored Troops, were reformed into two Cavalry troops, the ninth and tenth U.S. Cavalry, and eventually into two black infantry regiments, the twenty-fourth and twenty-fifth, which came to be known as the Buffalo Soldiers.

1866 — The Black Codes surfaced. These state laws passed in the United States after the Civil War were aimed at limiting the civil rights and civil liberties of blacks.

1876–1965 — The Jim Crow laws were in effect. They were state and local laws in the United States that mandated *de jure* racial segregation in all public facilities in southern states of the former Confederacy, with, starting in 1890, a "separate but equal" status for African Americans. The separation in practice led to conditions for African Americans that tended to be inferior to those provided for white Americans.

1879 — Blacks began to migrate in great numbers from the South, many to the Midwest. Cities like Chicago doubled its black population every ten years: 1870, 1880, and 1890.

1881 — The first Jim Crow laws segregating railroad coaches were passed by Tennessee, later by Florida, and then Texas.

1881 — Tuskegee Institute, headed by Booker T. Washington, was founded.

1882–1892 — Lynchings of blacks increased. More than 1,400 known instances occurred in this decade.

1895 — Booker T. Washington attained national prominence for his Atlanta Address.

1898 — Literacy tests and poll taxes to keep blacks from voting were upheld: *Williams v. Mississippi.*

1903 — The General Education Board, which was endowed by John D. Rockefeller, supported better instruction for teachers of black schools in the South.

1905 — W.E.B. Du Bois founded the Niagara Movement and had a Niagara Conference to urge equal civil and economic rights, better education, justice for blacks, and an end to segregation.

1909 — The National Association for the Advancement of Colored People (NAACP) was formed.

1910 — The National Urban League was founded to help blacks who were migrating to cities deal with social and economic issues.

1920–1930 — The Harlem Renaissance, a black cultural movement, burgeoned in the decade.

1924 — The Ku Klux Klan grew from an estimated one hundred thousand members in 27 states to an estimated four to four-and-a-half million members by 1924.

1927 — The Texas law that kept blacks from voting in Democratic elections was overturned by the Supreme Court: *Nixon v. Herndon.*

1935 — Harlem riots end with three killed and as much as $2 million in damages.

1936 — In the Summer Olympics in Berlin, Jesse Owens won four gold medals in track and field events.

1941 — On June 25, President Franklin D. Roosevelt issued Executive Order 8802, forbidding discrimination in employment in government and defense industries.

1941–1960 — Black migration continued, with 43 cities outside the South doubling their black population.

1942 — The Congress of Racial Equality (CORE) was founded by James Farmer.

1943 — Race riots occurred in Detroit, Michigan, and Mobile, Alabama, over employment of blacks.

1946 — On December 5, President Harry Truman issued Executive Order 9802 creating the Presidential Committee on Civil Rights.

1948 — President Truman's Executive Order 9981 barred segregation in the armed forces and barred discrimination in federal civil service positions.

1951 — On July 12, rioting in Cicero, Illinois, over segregated housing led to the National Guard being called out.

1952 — Ralph Ellison's *The Invisible Man* was published, addressing many of the social and intellectual issues facing African Americans early in the twentieth century.

1954 — The Little Rock Crisis occurred. On May 17, the U.S. Supreme Court ruled in *Brown v. Topeka Board of Education* that segregated schools are "inherently unequal." In September 1957, as a result of that ruling, nine African American students enrolled at Central High School in Little Rock, Arkansas.

1955 — On December 1, Rosa Parks refused a bus driver order to give up her seat to a white passenger.

1955 — The Montgomery Bus Boycott, led by Martin Luther King, Jr., took place.

1957 — Martin Luther King, Jr., along with Ralph Abernathy and other civil rights activists, helped found the Southern Christian Leadership Conference (SCLC), with King serving as its first president. The group was created to harness the moral authority and organizing power of black churches to conduct nonviolent protests in the service of civil rights reform. King led the SCLC until his death.

1958 — On September 20, while signing copies of his book *Stride Toward Freedom* in Blumstein's department store in Harlem, King narrowly escaped death when Izola Curry, a mentally ill black woman who believed he was conspiring against her with communists, stabbed him in the chest with a letter opener. After emergency surgery, King was hospitalized for several weeks, while Curry was found mentally incompetent to stand trial.

1959 — Martin Luther King, Jr. published a short book called *The Measure of a Man*, which contained his sermons "What Is Man?" and "The Dimensions of a Complete Life." The sermons argued for man's need for God's love and criticized the racial injustices of Western civilization.

1960 — On February 1, a sit-in at an F.W. Woolworth lunch counter in Greensboro, North Carolina, reflected the growing national movement of nonviolent protest.

1961 — Freedom riders were civil rights activists who rode interstate buses into the segregated southern United States in 1961 and following years to challenge the nonenforcement of the U.S. Supreme Court decisions *Irene Morgan v. Commonwealth of Virginia* (1946) and *Boyton v. Virginia* (1960), which ruled that segregated public buses were unconstitutional.

1961 — In November was the Albany Movement—a desegregation coalition formed in Albany, Georgia. In December, Martin Luther King, Jr. and the SCLC became involved.

1963 — In April, the SCLC began a campaign against racial segregation and economic injustice in Birmingham, Alabama. The campaign used nonviolent but intentionally confrontational tactics, developed in part by Rev. Wyatt Tee Walker. Black people in Birmingham, organizing with the SCLC, occupied public spaces with marches and sit-ins, openly violating laws that they considered unjust.

1963 — On June 12, a Mississippi desegregation leader, Medgar Evans, was killed by gunfire in Jackson, Mississippi.

1963 — On June 11, John F. Kennedy called for a Civil Rights Act in his civil rights speech. He asked for legislation "giving all Americans the right to be served in facilities which are open to the public—hotels, restaurants, theaters, retail stores, and similar establishments"—as well as "greater protection for the right to vote." Kennedy delivered this speech following a series of protests from the African American community, the most concurrent being the Birmingham campaign, which concluded in May 1963.

1963 — On August 28 was the March on Washington—one of the largest political rallies for human rights in U.S. history. It called for civil and economic rights for African Americans.

1963 — The FBI, under a written directive from Attorney General Robert F. Kennedy, began tapping King's telephone in the fall. Concerned that allegations of communists in the SCLC would derail the administration's civil rights initiatives if made public, Kennedy warned King to discontinue the suspect associations. He later felt compelled to issue the written directive authorizing the FBI to wiretap King and other SCLC leaders. J. Edgar Hoover feared Communists were trying to infiltrate the civil rights movement, but when no such evidence emerged, the bureau used the incidental details caught on tape over the next five years in attempts to force King out of the preeminent leadership position.

1963 — On November 22, John F. Kennedy was assassinated while in a motorcade in Dallas, Texas.

1964 — King and the SCLC were driving forces behind intense demonstrations in St. Augustine, Florida. The movement marched nightly through the city and suffered violent attacks from white supremacists. Hundreds of the marchers were arrested and jailed.

1964 — On June 21, three civil rights workers participating in the "Mississippi Freedom Summer"—James Earl Chaney, Andrew Goodman, and Michael "Mickey" Schwerner—disappeared in Neshoba County, Mississippi, getting national media attention and prompting the FBI to send more than a hundred agents to investigate. Public outcry hastened passage of the Civil Rights Act. The search for the three civil rights workers lasted forty-four days before their bodies were unearthed.

1964 — The Civil Rights Act, enacted on July 2, 1964, was signed into law by President Johnson, despite opposition from southern Republicans and Democrats and a 54-day filibuster. The law outlawed major forms of discrimination against racial, ethnic, national and religious minorities, and women.

1964 — On October 14, Martin Luther King, Jr. received the Nobel Peace Prize for combating racial inequality through nonviolence.

1964 — In December 1964, King and the SCLC joined forces with the Student Nonviolent Coordinating Committee (SNCC) in Selma, Alabama, where the SNCC had been working on voter registration for several months. A local judge issued an injunction that barred any gathering of three or more people affiliated with the SNCC, SCLC, DCVL, or any of forty-one named civil rights leaders. This injunction temporarily halted civil rights activity until King defied it by speaking at Brown Chapel on January 2, 1965.

1965 — On February 21, Malcolm X, an African American Muslim minister and human rights activist, was assassinated by Ku Klux Klan gunfire.

1965 — On March 7, King, James Bevel, and the SCLC, in partial collaboration with the SNCC, attempted to organize a march from Selma to the state capital of Montgomery. The first attempt to march on March 7 was aborted because of mob and police violence against the demonstrators. This day has since become known as Bloody Sunday. Bloody Sunday was a major turning point in the effort to gain public support for the civil rights movement, the clearest demonstration up to that time of the dramatic potential of King's nonviolence strategy.

1965 — The Voting Rights Act was sent to Congress by President Johnson on March 17, 1965. On August 6, President Johnson signed the Act into law.

1965–1967 — Thurgood Marshall was appointed Solicitor General of the United States and in 1967 became a justice of the Supreme Court. Robert Weaver was named Secretary of Housing and Urban Development, while Andrew Brimmer became a member of the Federal Reserve Board.

1966 — The Black Power Movement took place. Stokely Carmichael saw King's nonviolence as a tactic rather than as a principle. He was critical of civil rights leaders who called for the integration of African Americans into the mainstream middle class.

1966 — The Black Panthers, a revolutionary party, was founded by Bobby Seale and Huey P. Newton. Many of its leaders were killed or imprisoned in the subsequent violent confrontations with police.

1966 — When the Meredith Mississippi March Against Fear passed through Grenada, Mississippi, on June 15, 1966, it sparked months of civil rights activity on the part of Grenada blacks. They formed the Grenada County Freedom Movement (GCFM) as an SCLC affiliate, and within days 1,300 blacks registered to vote.

1966 — After several successes in the South, King and others in the civil rights organizations tried to spread the movement to the North, with Chicago as their first destination. King and Ralph Abernathy, both from the middle class, moved into a building at 1550 South Hamlin Avenue, in the slums of North Lawndale on the west side of Chicago, as an educational experience and to demonstrate their support and empathy for the poor.

1967 — In an April 4 appearance at the New York City Riverside Church—exactly one year before his death—King delivered a speech titled "Beyond Vietnam." He spoke strongly against the U.S. role in the war and said the U.S. Congress was spending more and more on the military and less and less on antipoverty programs at the same time.

1968 — Eldridge Cleaver's *Soul on Ice* was published. A post-prison book, the central premise is the trouble of "identification as a black soul which has been 'colonized'…by an oppressive white society."

1968 — King and the SCLC organized the "Poor People's Campaign" to address issues of economic justice.

1968 — On April 3, Dr. King delivered his last sermon, "I've Been to the Mountaintop" at Mason Temple, the International Headquarters of The Church of God In Christ.

1968 — On April 4 at 6:01 p.m., a shot rang out as Martin Luther King, Jr. stood on the Lorraine Motel's second-floor balcony in Memphis. He was pronounced dead at St. Joseph's Hospital.

1968 — The plan to set up a shantytown in Washington, D.C. was carried out soon after the April 4 assassination. Criticism of King's plan was subdued in the wake of his death, and the SCLC received an unprecedented wave of donations for the purpose of carrying it out. The campaign officially began in Memphis, on May 2, at the hotel where King was murdered. Thousands of demonstrators arrived on the National Mall and established a camp they called "Resurrection City." They stayed for six weeks.

1968 — On October 16 at the Olympics in Mexico City, African American track and field athletes Tommie Smith and John Carlos, who had won gold and silver medals in the 200-meter race, raised black-gloved fists into the air and held them there during the length of the "Star Spangled Banner." Smith later said the gesture was not intended as a black power salute but as a human rights salute. The two athletes were expelled from the games.

1968 — In the November 5 presidential election, 51.4% of registered nonwhites voted, as compared to 44% in 1964, while black registration for voting in 11 southern states rose from 1,463,000 in 1960 to 3,449,000 in 1971.

1970–1973 — Black migration reversed from the North back to the South, reflecting economic factors.

ENDNOTES

1   Segal, Ronald, *The Black Diaspora: Five Centuries of the Black Experience Outside Africa*. New York: Farrar, Straus and Giroux, 1995.

2   Fogel, Robert William, and Stanley L. Engerman, *The Economics of American Negro Slavery*. New York: W. W. Norton & Company, 1974.

3   *Ibid*.

4   http://www.justice.gov/crt/about/vot/intro/intro_c.php

5   http://www.dol.gov/_sec/media/reports/blacklaborforce/

6   http://inbizdev.wordpress.com/wealth/

7   DiTomaso, Nancy, *The American Non-Dilemma: Racial Inequality Without Racism* (CUP Services, 2012).

8   Stainback, Kevin, and Donald Tomaskovic Devey, *Documenting Desegregation: Racial and Gender Segregation in Private-Sector Employment Since the Civil Rights Act* (Russell Sage Foundation, 2012).

SOUTHERN CHRISTIAN LEADERSHIP CONFERENCE

The very beginnings of the SCLC can be traced back to the Montgomery Bus Boycott. The boycott began on December 5, 1955 after Rosa Parks was arrested for refusing to give up her seat to a white man on the bus. The boycott lasted for 381 days and ended on December 21, 1956, with the desegregation of the Montgomery bus system. The boycott was carried out by the newly established Montgomery Improvement Association (MIA). Martin Luther King, Jr. served as President and Ralph David Abernathy served as Program Director. It was one of history's most dramatic and massive nonviolent protests, stunning the nation and the world.

The boycott was also a signal to Black America to begin a new phase of the long struggle, a phase that came to be known as the modern civil rights movement. As bus boycotts spread across the South, leaders of the MIA and other protest groups met in Atlanta on January 10–11, 1957, to form a regional organization and coordinate protest activities across the South.

Despite a bombing of the home and church of Ralph David Abernathy during the Atlanta meeting, 60 people from 10 states assembled and announced the founding of the Southern Leadership Conference on Transportation and Nonviolent Integration. They issued a document declaring that civil rights are essential to democracy, that segregation must end, and that all Black people should reject segregation absolutely and nonviolently.

They further organized at a meeting in New Orleans, Louisiana on February 14, 1957. The organization shortened its name to Southern Leadership Conference, established an Executive Board of Directors, and elected officers, including Dr. Martin Luther King, Jr. as President, Dr. Ralph David Abernathy as Financial Secretary-Treasurer, Rev. C.K. Steele of Tallahassee, Florida as Vice President, Rev. T.J. Jemison of Baton Rouge, Louisiana as Secretary, and Attorney I.M. Augustine of New Orleans, Louisiana as General Counsel.

At its first convention in Montgomery in August 1957, the Southern Leadership Conference adopted its current name, the Southern Christian Leadership Conference. Basic decisions made by the founders at these early meetings included the adoption of non-violent mass action as the cornerstone of strategy, the affiliation of local community organizations with SCLC across the South, and a determination to make the SCLC movement open to all, regardless of race, religion, or background.

SCLC is a now a nationwide organization made up of chapters and affiliates with programs that affect the lives of all Americans: north, south, east, and west. Its sphere of influence and interests has become international in scope because the human rights movement transcends national boundaries.

BOB ADELMAN
Documentary Photographer &
Book Producer
Website: bobadelman.net

MAGAZINES: Photographs for Cover Stories: *Esquire, TIME, People, LIFE, New York, Harper's, Newsweek, New York Times Magazine, Fortune, American Heritage, The London Times Magazine, Stern, Look, Paris Match,* USIA Publications.

BOOKS PHOTOGRAPHED AND PRODUCED: *Down Home; On and Off the Street; Street Smart; Gentleman of Leisure; Ladies of the Night; Out of Left Field,* all with Susan Hall; *The Next America* with Michael Harrington; *The Reagan Report; It Grows on You: A Hair Raising Survey of Human Plumage* with Roy Blount Jr.; *The Art of Roy Lichtenstein,* essay by Calvin Tompkins, photographs and interview by Bob Adelman; *Carver Country: The World of Raymond Carver,* introduction by Tess Gallagher; *Visions of Liberty: The Bill of Rights For All Americans* by Ira Glasser, photographs by Bob Adelman; *King: The Photobiography of Martin Luther King Jr.* by Charles

Johnson and Bob Adelman; *Mine Eyes Have Seen: Bearing Witness to the Struggle for Civil Rights,* essays by Charles Johnson, photographs by Bob Adelman; *New York Times* Book Company: developed and photographed the Sidewalk Reading program; Holt, Rinehart and Winston, Random House, Dell Publishing: preparation of educational material.

BOOKS PRODUCED: *Pollock Painting,* photographs by Hans Namuth; *Bruce Davidson Photographs; Brancusi Photographs; Sculptor's Drawings; Arsenal of Democracy* by Tom Gervasi; *Soviet Military Power: The Annotated and Corrected Version of the Pentagon's Guide* by Tom Gervasi; *The Film Encyclopedia* by Ephriam Katz; *Pictures Under Discussion; LIFE Classic Photographs; LIFE Faces; Celebrating the Negative; LIFE Photographers: What They Saw,* all by John Loengard; *Born to Run Things: An Utterly Unauthorized Biography of George Bush* by Tony Hendra; *Grace: An Intimate Portrait of Princess Grace* by Howell Conant; *Brad '61: Portrait of the Artist as a Young Man, An Original Romance* by Tony Hendra, Inspired by the Pop Paintings of Roy Lichtenstein; *Tijuana Bibles: Art and Wit in America's Forbidden Funnies, 1930s-1950s* by Bob Adelman, commentary by Richard Merkin, introduction by Art Spiegelman; *The London Sunday Times 1000 Makers of the Cinema; Roy Lichtenstein's ABC* by Bob Adelman; *Magic*

Movie Moments by Bob Adelman, Michael Rand, and George Perry, introduction by Terry Gilliam; *Sinatra: An Intimate Portrait of a Very Good Year*, photographs by John Dominis, text by Richard B. Stolley; *Remembering Jack* by Jacques Lowe, text by Hugh Sidey; *LIFE: The Great Photographers* by the editors of *LIFE*; *As I See It* by John Loengard, introduction by Ann Beattie; *LIFE: Remembering Grace*; *LIFE: Remembering Martin Luther King Jr.*

TEACHING: International Center for Photography, The New School, School of Visual Arts. Lectured at Columbia University, Stanford University, Union College, Philadelphia College of Art, University of Minnesota, Miami University, Ohio State University, Steamboat Falls Workshop, Boston Museum of Fine Arts.

PORTFOLIOS: Camera, Popular Photography Annual, Photo, My Brother's Keeper.

AWARDS: Guggenheim Fellowship; National Endowment for the Arts Grant; Art Director's Club Awards: New York, Washington, San Francisco; American Institute of Graphic Arts 50 Books Awards; University of Missouri School of Journalism.

EXHIBITS: Smithsonian Museum, Martha Jackson Gallery, Margaret Mitchell House, American Federation of the Arts, Martin Luther King Jr. National Historic Site, Howard Greenberg Gallery, Westwood Gallery, Boca Raton Museum of Fine Arts, High Museum. Photographs in the Collections of the Museum of Modern Art, Getty Museum, High Museum, Hallmark Collection, Boca Raton Museum & private collections.

EDUCATION: B.A., Rutgers; Law Studies, Harvard; M.A. Philosophy, Columbia

MARCH
Graphic Novel Excerpt

Many Marched. Congressman John Lewis, one of the architects and keynote speakers of the March on Washington, is presenting his life and memories of the movement for new generations in a trilogy of graphic novels entitled MARCH. For more information, visit www.topshelfcomix.com/march.

103

Many were arrested. From the streets to jail cells, Congressman John Lewis depicts scenes from the march, presenting his life and memories of the movement for new generations. Visit www.topshelfcomix.com/march.